My Cat Is Hiding

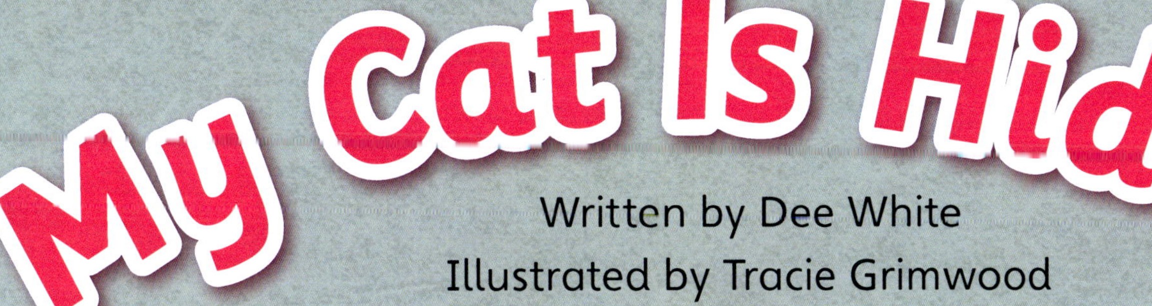

Written by Dee White
Illustrated by Tracie Grimwood

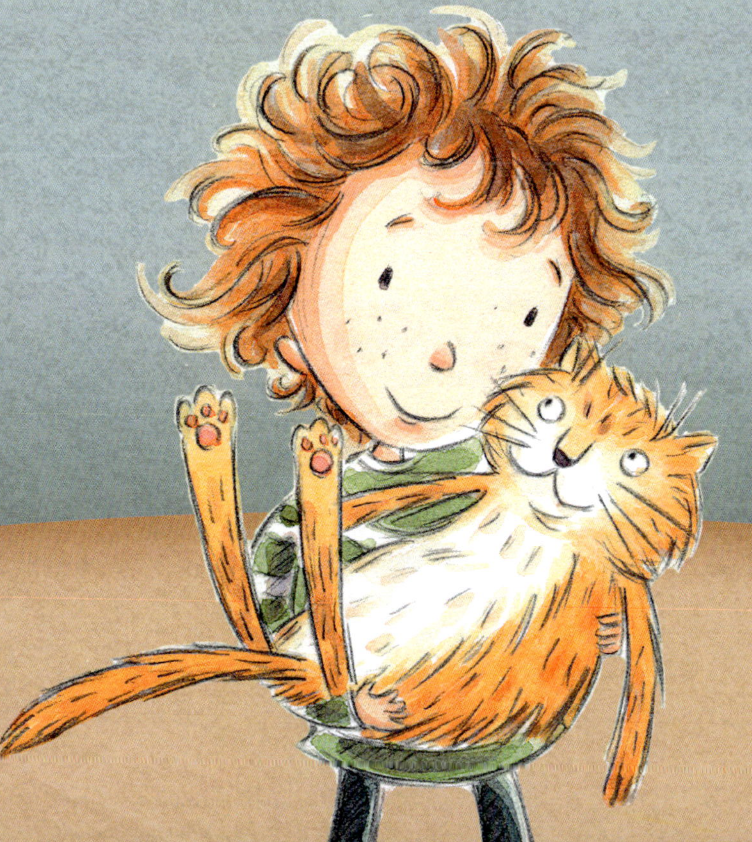

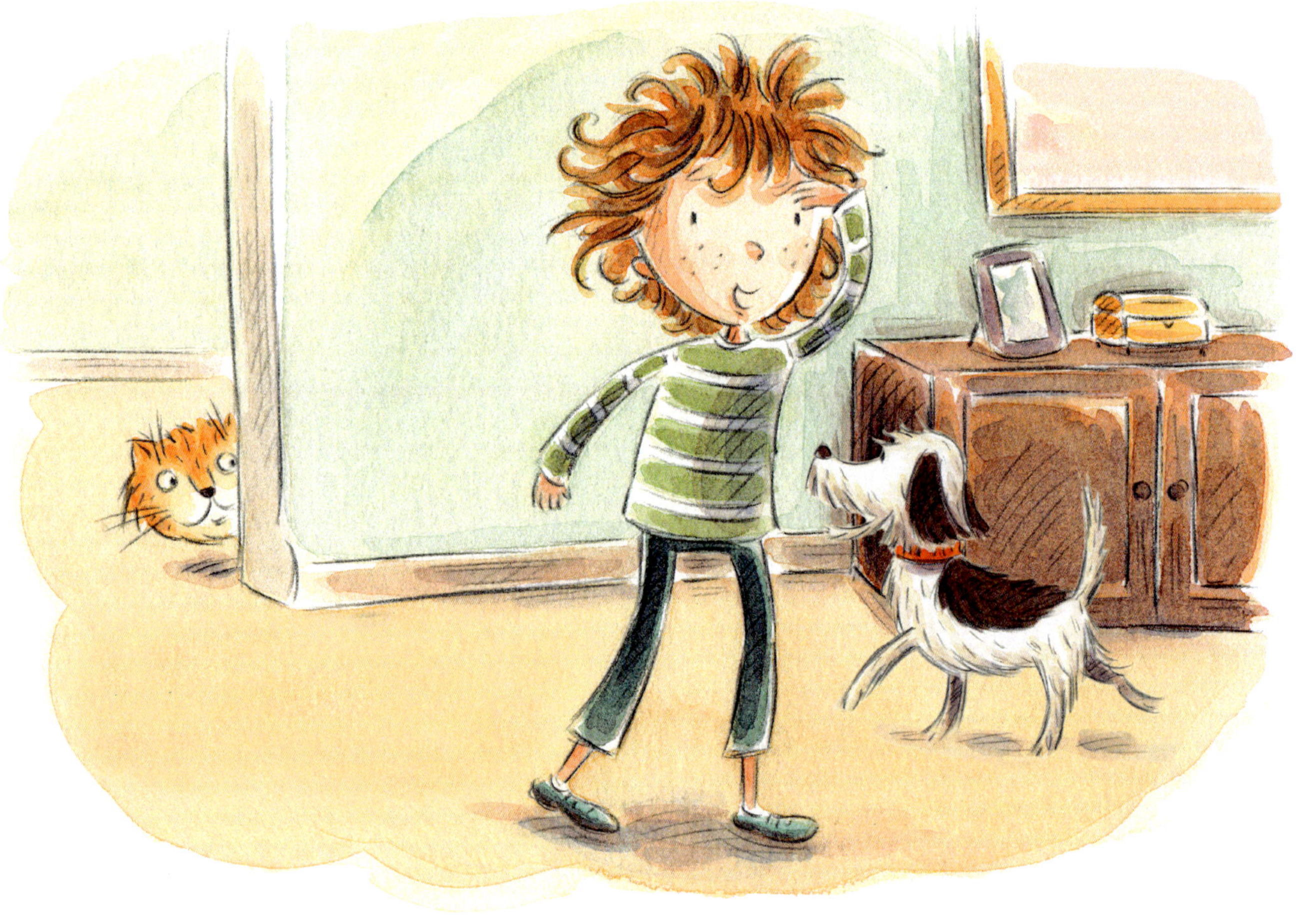

My cat is hiding.

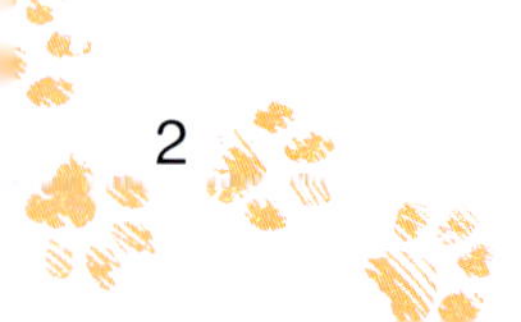

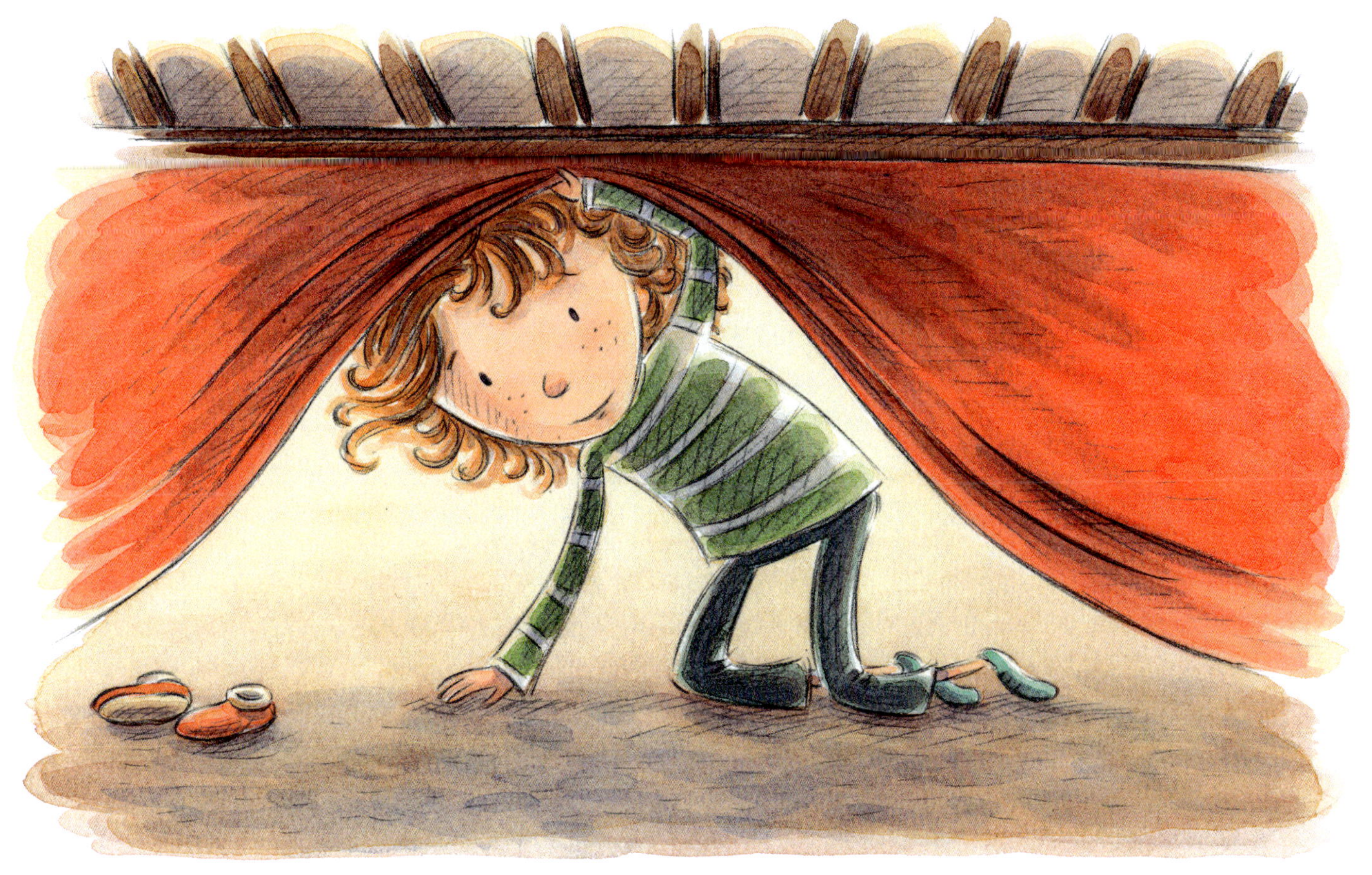

Is she under the bed?

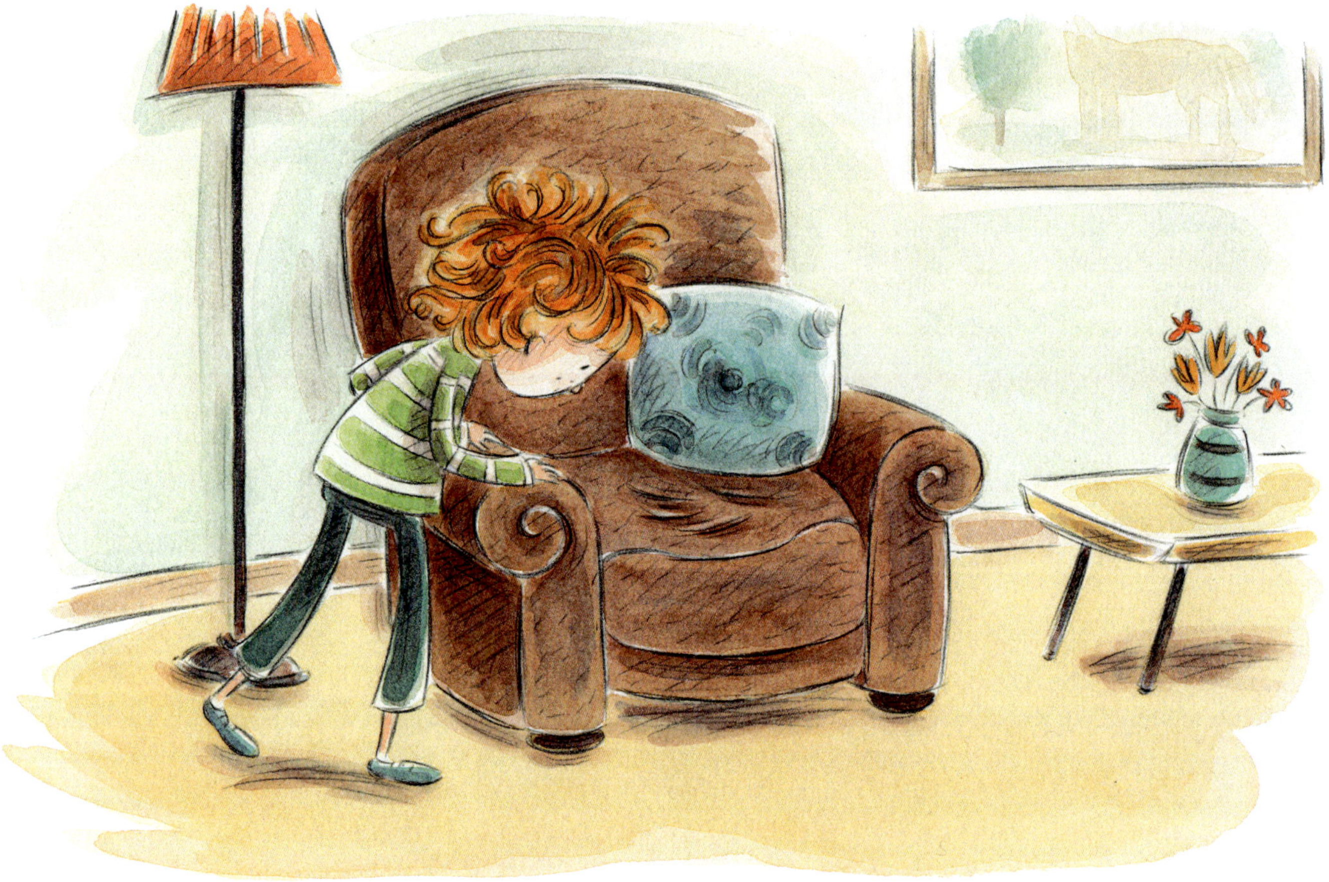

Is she on the chair?

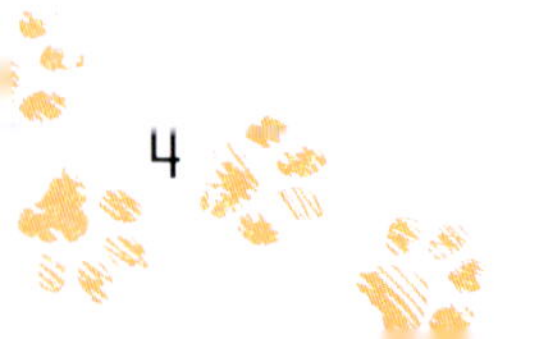

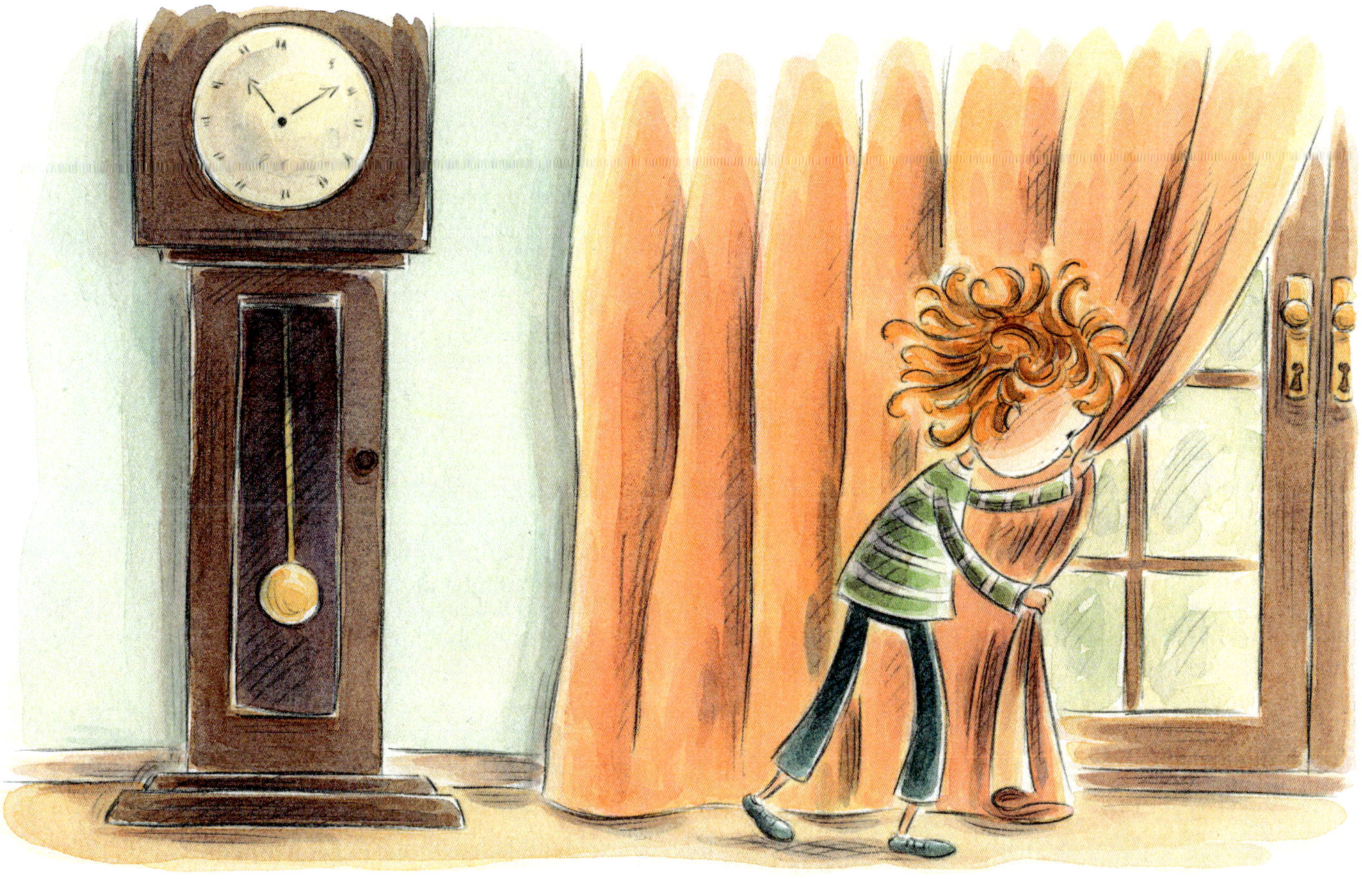

Is she behind the curtain?

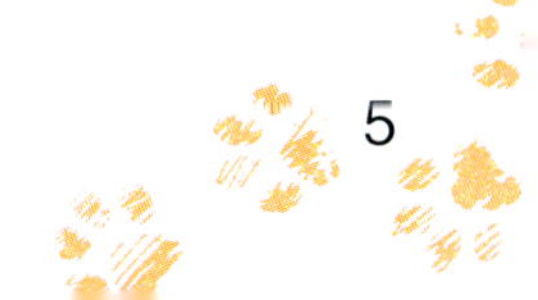

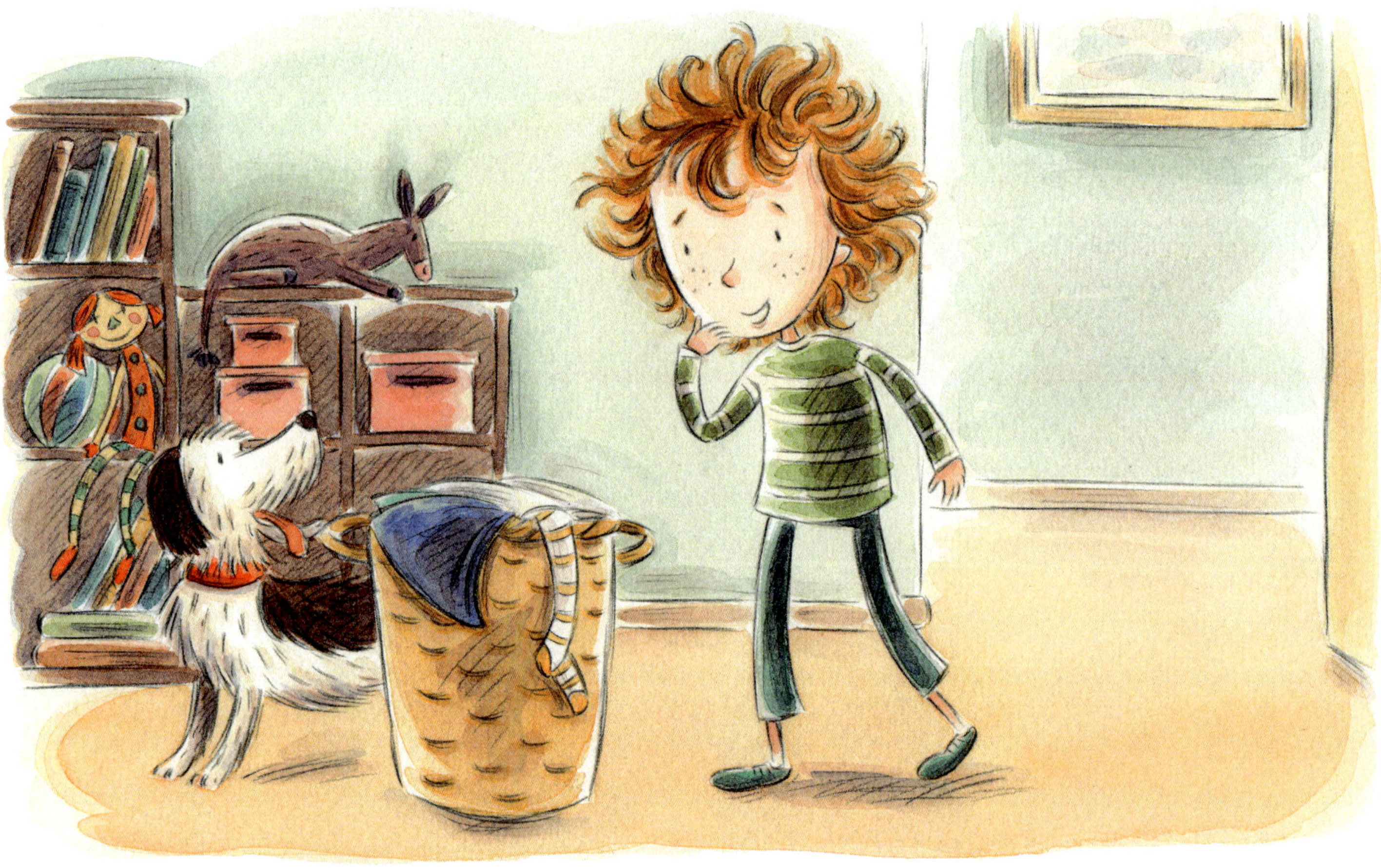

Is she in the basket?

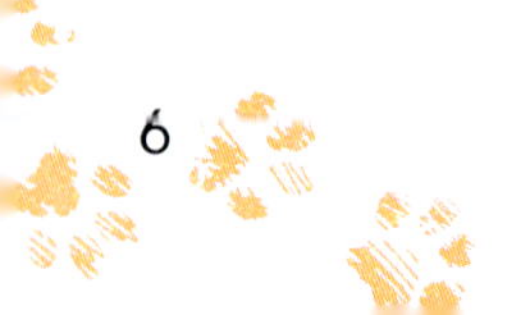

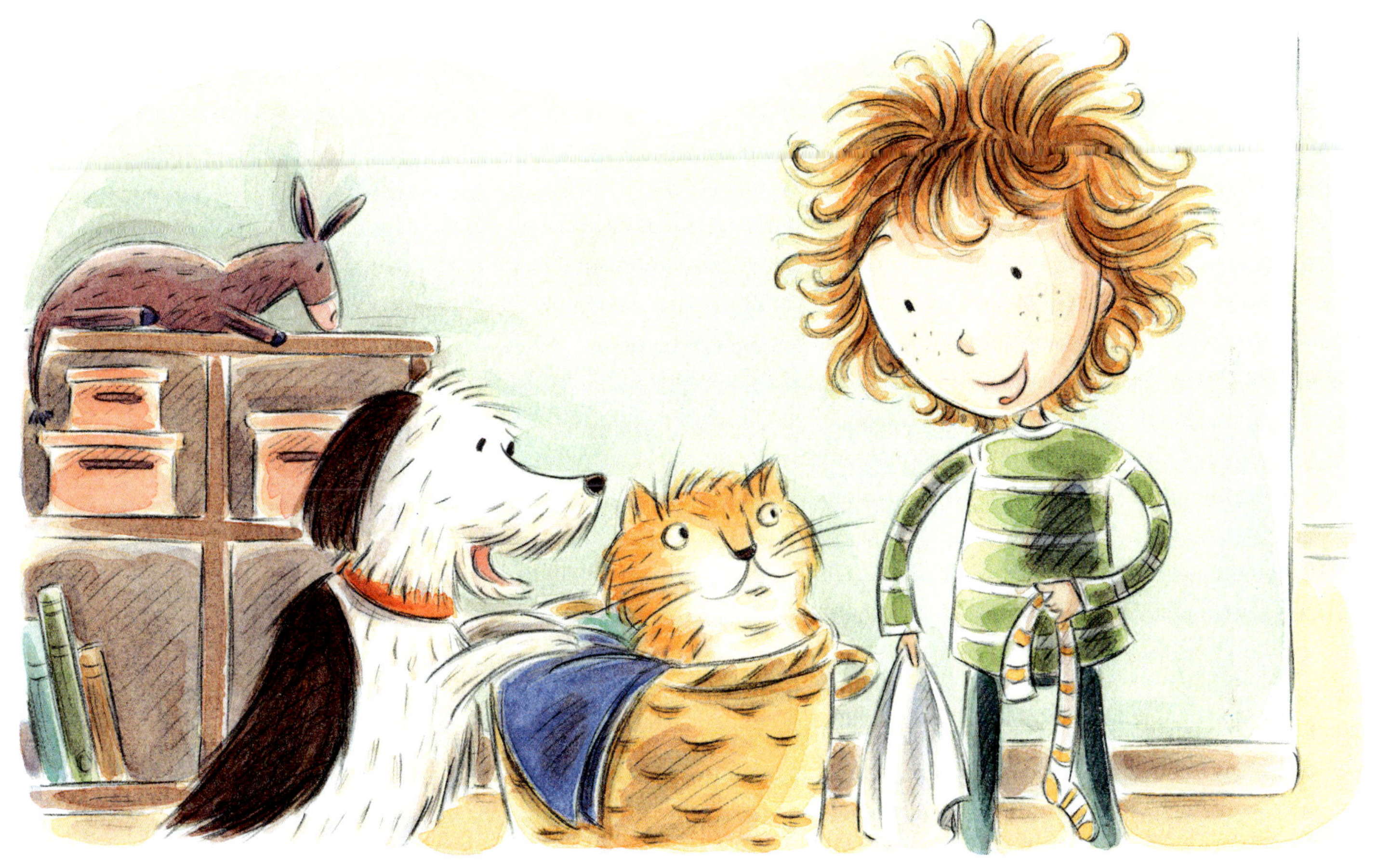

Here she is!

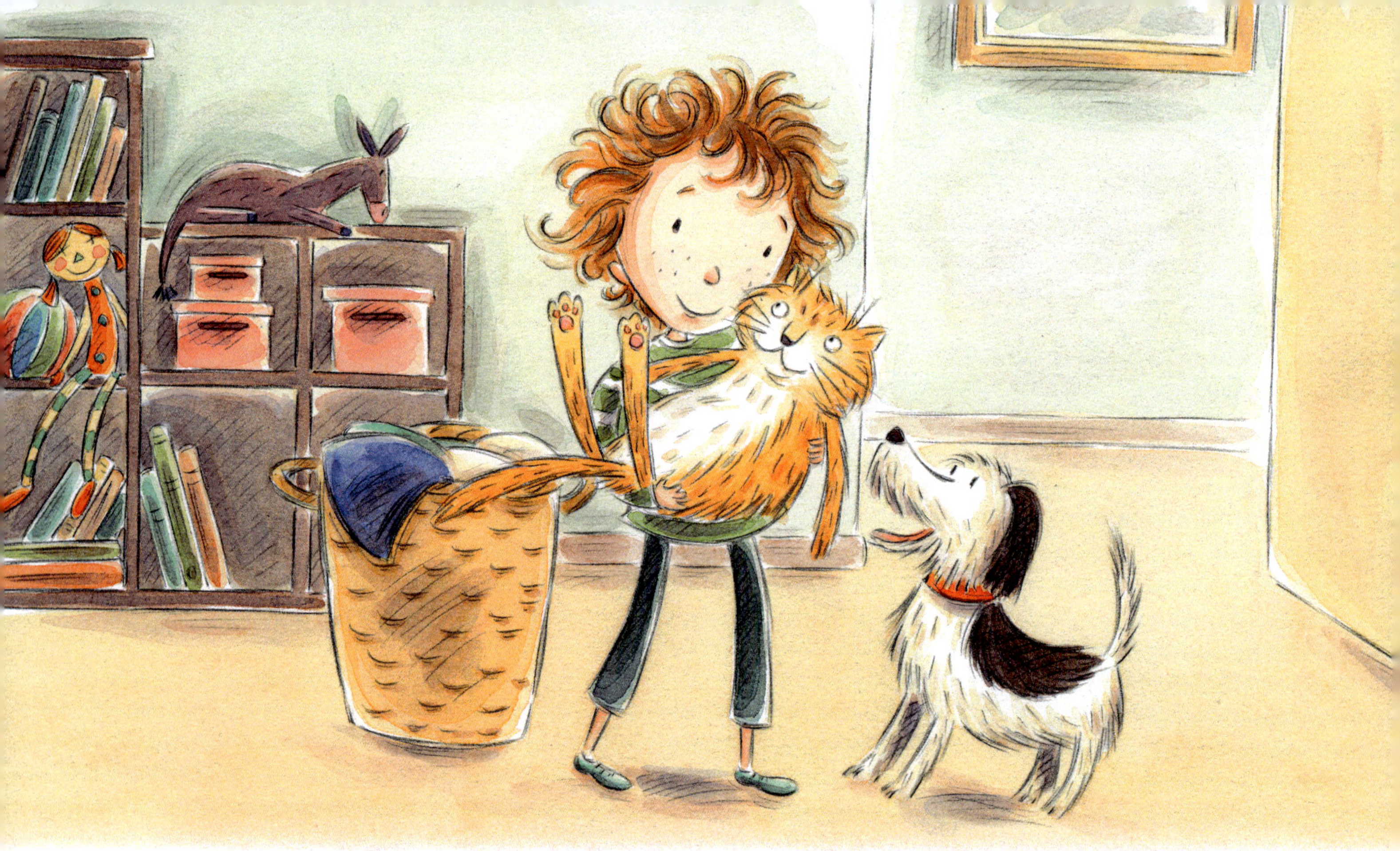

She was hiding from the dog!

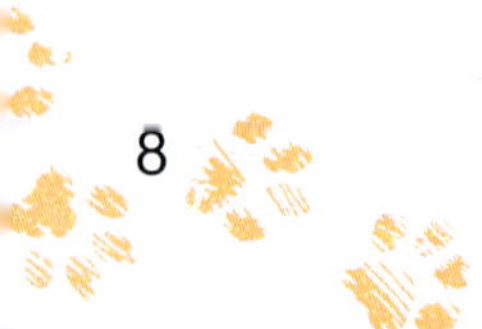